God's Purpose
FOR MY PAIN
In Memory of My Beloved Son, JaRon E. Collins

LOSSIE M. DAVIS

Copyright 2016 Lossie M. Davis, All rights reserved.

No part of this book may be reproduced, stored in a retrieval system, or transmitted by any means without the written permission of the author.

Scripture quotations noted are from the New King James Version of the Holy Bible

Table of Contents

Dedication
Preface
Introduction   i

Chapter 1
The Battle Is Not Yours   1

Chapter 2
Trusting God In The Storm   6

Chapter 3
The Journey Continues   11

Chapter 4
The Struggle Is Real   18

Chapter 5
Restored Peace   22

Chapter 6
Reflections   27

ONLY GOD.

Because He Doesn't Put More On Us Than We Can Bare!

LOVE- unconditional
LOSS- unbelievable
LAW- undeniably justifiable

Dedication

God's Purpose For My Pain is dedicated to my youngest son, JaRon E. Collins who is resting in peace with our Heavenly Father. I thank God and give Him all glory, honor and praise for choosing me to be his mother. You are now my Guardian Angel, smiling down from heaven.

To my first born son Jovaris, I thank God for allowing you to be a very big part of my life every day. You have always made me so proud the way you strive to be the best son, father, nephew, friend, and role model that you can be. I know you have been through a lot; however, just continue to keep God first in your life and everything else will go according to HIS will. Remember that the sky is the limit and that God has blessed you with so many gifts; continue to utilize them for HIS glory. I love you will all my heart.

To my husband, Pastor Darryl E. Davis Sr. God blessed me with you, a God fearing man who loves God first and then God's people. You have been a great inspiration to me and have helped me so much spiritually in my walk with the Lord. You have loved me in spite of me with all my flaws, and for that I say thank you. I love you with all my heart.

To my family, friends, law enforcement family, church family and everyone in my inner circle that prayed for me, encouraged me and supported me through this very difficult time in the loss of my son. Words are inadequate to truly express my heartfelt thoughts, but God knows that I could not have made it without you. Thank you for being there, when I didn't even know you were there, too weak to lift my head and respond because of the pain and trauma I was experiencing from knowing that JaRon was dead and I would never be able to touch or see him again. No mother should have to endure such hurt. I love you all for being there for me and not giving up on me, when life got so hard that I wanted to give up on myself and had no more fight in me.

God is an awesome God and knows who to send in the time of need.

In Luke 4:18 Jesus tells us that He comes to heal the broken hearted. My heart was broken and crushed after the death of JaRon. I never thought I would be able to live a normal life again without daily crying and hurting and struggling…..but GOD! Some days are harder than others as I look back over where

God has brought me from, I'm grateful and thankful. But, when you carry a child for 9-months, then have to bury him 17 years later, it is a loss like no other. The natural process of life says that children should be burying their parents, not parents burying their children. This is happening more and more every day due to the unnecessary violence that only God can make stop.

Now, my healing is God breathed as I walk this daily journey and understand more, GOD'S PURPOSE FOR MY PAIN!

Preface

This book is a testimony to what God will do in the midst of. This story to tell was ordained by God, journaled by a mother in her time of hurt and pain to release and grow from a tragedy that had she been given the choice, she would not have been a part of; and, written from the pen of a god mother who was blessed to be a help, influence and second-mother to a son who she did not birth, but was loaned to her by God and his mother, until such a time as this.

This reflection of a little boy who had a contagious smile that would light up the world, who would cuddle up to you, look up with those Big brown eyes and say I love you with a tone that would make you melt like cubed ice on a hot summer day.

JaRon, only a kindergartner at the time, would be ready to fight my youngest daughter Portland, for his "rightful" place, as close to me as possible, on the couch watching television, in the kitchen making dinner, or in the car, and neither of them were old enough or allowed to ride in the front seat with me.

I thank God and this awesome mother, my sister, my friend, my son's mother – Lossie M. Davis for giving me the son I never had and for trusting me to love JaRon and help raise him, until such a time as this.

From one mother to another, JaRon's legacy must continue as we write his story. Only God knows why? I love you always, Marta E. Bell

GOD'S PURPOSE FOR MY PAIN

God's Purpose

FOR MY PAIN

In Memory of My Beloved Son

JaRon E. Collins

"The Rising Star"

October 23, 1993 – July 30, 2011

Introduction

Only God could give me the healing I needed to make me whole again.

There is a purpose for my Pain. My self-confidence as a mother and a woman of God were at an all-time low. I had to ask God was I being punished for my past sins? I've struggled with a lot of issues in my life like everyone else. Why was I being punished? Did I not pray enough? Should I have given God more of my time in praise and worship? I know that everything in this life has a purpose. There are no mistakes; all events are blessings and lessons given to us to learn from. Learn to get in touch with the silence within yourself. Moreover, trust God in your storm. There is a purpose for all pain and God is not a God of punishment.

Now faith is the substance of things hoped for and the evidence of things not seen. (Hebrews 11:1)

I felt my trust in God was lost, although I thought I had followed what Gods word says to do. It was as though God failed; but, God says He can do everything but fail.

No matter what happens in your life, God can restore. Be anxious for nothing, but in everything by prayer and supplication, with thanksgiving, let your requests be made known to God; and the peace of God, which surpasses all understanding, will guard your hearts and minds through Christ Jesus. (Philippians 4:6-8)

THE BATTLE IS NOT YOURS

For you have armed me with strength for the battle; you have subdued under me those who rose up against me (Psalms 18:39)

My story I share will contain details about how I dealt with shock, numbness, sadness, fear, anger and frustration and ultimately, trusting God through the storm.

My Storm began on July 30, 2011 at approximately 8:30 a.m. I received a loud knock on my door and unbeknownst to me that this loud knock on that early morning would change my life forever. I was asleep, and once I finally got myself together I looked out the window to see who was knocking at my door like "The Police". As an Officer myself, I knew and recognized the sound that I had delivered to other's doors when duty called….. knock loud and hard so you will be heard; well, I was sleeping very sound and this loud knock did not go unheard. Looking out the window, I could see two unmarked police cars and I just figured they were coming to notify me of something that was going on in the neighborhood. In my mind I had already conjured up that thought, that the knock was nothing pertaining to me, my household or my family. Once I opened the door, the first person I saw was the Indianapolis Metropolitan Police Department Chaplain Laverne Sandborn and she was crying. I'm standing there trying to figure out, but couldn't understand for the life of me what she was crying for; so, I asked her what was going on? She said "can I come in and talk to you?" I said sure, come in please. She then asked me to come and sit down because she had some bad news to tell me. I replied "no Chaplain", I don't want to sit down, please just tell me while I'm standing here. The next devastating words that came out of her mouth were that there had been an accident and my son had been shot. Now, I have two sons, Jovaris who is my oldest son that lives in Indianapolis where I live, he was 25 years old at the time; and then, there's JaRon, my youngest son who was 17 years old and away from Indianapolis in Tennessee attending a basketball camp. So, in my mind I just know JaRon is okay and safe. My next question to Chaplain Sanborn was what happened? who shot Jovaris? and is he okay. Chaplain Sanborn said NO Lossie, it's not Jovaris, its JaRon and He is NOT okay, HE IS DEAD!

DEAD! I repeated what I just heard, to make sure I was not only wide awake; but, that I had heard her correctly. For clarification I repeated it again, DEAD! I just couldn't wrap my mind around what could have happened. How could something like this happen to my son and me? I IMMEDIATELY went into total shock and disbelief. My body was completely numb and I didn't remember anything after that; other than what I was later told. That 911 had to be called and an ambulance dispatched to my residence because I passed completely out and that the paramedics had to use that "smelly" stuff to bring me back to consciousness.

From the time I was brought back to consciousness and the next passing hours I kept trying to figure out why and how this could happen to me. I kept talking to God saying "Lord, I'm a good person" a great mother and I'm a Faithful Christian. All I wanted to know was WHY?

I was always told to never question God's work; but, I needed answers. The devil spoke to me and said "see God don't love you". "See what He allowed to happen to your son" "Now you need to kill the person that killed your son". So, the next question that came out of my mouth was, Why God? Why Me? Why did you let something as tragic as this happen to my son? He didn't deserve this, he was just a baby he hadn't lived his life yet. What am I going to do without him, my baby, my baby, that was my baby. God then spoke back to me plain as day and said Dear Child, I lost my only begotten son to so I feel your pain. You will get through this. I think at that point a light bulb came back on in my head because darkness was trying to take over. I was just sad, hurt, lost, confused, distraught, angry and frustrated all at the same time. I wasn't sure if I was going or coming……BUT GOD!

God spoke to me in such a powerful voice, that from that point on all I could do was cry and scream….Jesus, Jesus, Jesus, Help Me Lord Please, Help Me Lord Please because I can't get through this without You. You are going to have to help me ALL the way!

The tragic news began to circulate to family members, friends and my Law Enforcement family that I worked with, and people began to come to my home. I was told that there were so many people there to comfort and support me at my house, that the normal flow of traffic could not even get down my street. My brother Marcus and his family were already in town visiting from Milwaukee, so they were at my house. My oldest son Jovaris was notified of his brother's death. None of them that were trying to comfort me could help me deal with the pain I was feeling from the loss of my son being shot to death. I felt at the time that I was given this tragic news that I had died right along with my son because my body had no feeling, no life left in it, whatsoever. I started to feel as if I was having an out of body experience; an encounter that had me trying to bargain with God to take my life and let my son come back and live life because I wanted my son alive, NOT DEAD!

Now, I know death is final, but how would I ever be able to see my son again? Not thinking that if

I live right on this earth and do God's will, I would see my son again.

TRUSTING GOD IN THE STORM

Trust in the Lord with all your heart; And lean not on your own understanding (Proverbs 3:5)

Time had passed, and it is now the morning of August 1st, time for me and my family to head to Tennessee where my son JaRon had been murdered. There were funeral arrangements that had to be made and the dreadful task of meeting with the Detectives who were assigned to investigate JaRon's murder case. I'm lost, confused, overwhelmed, and don't know where to start or what to do. My mind and body had completely shut down. But, thanks be to God my Law Enforcement Family had me covered. Deputy Chief Eva Talley-Sanders of the Marion County Sheriff's Department made arrangements and allowed Captain Donald Vancleave to drive myself, my brother Marcus, my son Jovaris, and my best friend, Marta Bell who was a Detective with the Indianapolis Metropolitan Police Department, and also, she was JaRon's godmother to Dyersburg, Tennessee to begin handling the unwanted business of making funeral arrangements

Prior to traveling to Dyersburg, Tennessee, I had been informed of business that needed to be handled that were part of the process of preparing for burying my son. This process was unfamiliar to me and almost like a nightmare that I wanted to wake up from. I was advised that I not only needed to decide a funeral home in Tennessee to pick up my son's body; but, that I needed to provide clothing for him to wear to be buried in. Still in shock and denial, I heeded what I had been told, to bring a suit, shirt, tie, underclothes, belt, socks, shoes; oh how I wish this was a dream, a dress rehearsal for a stage play, not the reality of putting my son away. What a dreadful task, purchasing clothes for JaRon to be buried in.

No mother wants to pick out a suit for their son to be buried in; but, it had to be done, so, me, JaRon's godmother Marta and her oldest daughter Amethyst arrive at a store near Castleton Square Mall in Indianapolis, to meet with Mr. Dixon the funeral director; however, trying to match a blue suit and tie and shirt was not making sense to me. I kept breaking down in the store and nothing seemed appropriate and I began to scream, NO! NO! I should be buying him clothes to graduate in, or go to the prom in, not to wear in a casket "I can't do this" "I can't do this" Lord I need you, Lord I need you right now. I know people in that store thought I was crazy because everything they showed me to purchase I said no and hollered and cried. Eventually they brought me a chair and I just sat down near the dressing room and let Mr. Dixon, JaRon's god mother and his god sister Amethyst keep bringing me clothes until we made the final decision of what JaRon would be buried in.

Upon arrival to Dyersburg, Tennessee we met with Detective Jim Joyner and Lieutenant Billy Williams of the Dyersburg Police Department; only to be told that at that present time they did not have a suspect in JaRon's murder. No suspect-disappointing to say the least....BUT GOD! Trust Him in your storm.

The same day of meeting with the detectives, we then have to meet with the coaches and basketball team members in the gym at Ripley High School where JaRon had played basketball with his fellow team mates. They were so heart-broken over JaRon's death, a gym full of high school students crying in disbelief.

See, JaRon was a young man with a promising future, and a contagious smile. One of his favorite sayings was "Everybody Loves Me" and, everybody did. If you met JaRon once, you were hooked on his innocence and charming ways. Imagine, in my own pain of losing my son, I was asked to speak to these hurting, crying basketball teammates and school mates of his; so, I did. Only God knows how I got the strength to speak, but, I did to the best of my ability and made it through without having a nervous breakdown. When I finished speaking, it was the love and support of the entire basketball team and coaches that surrounded me and my family and all we could do was cry together. An unbelievable scene that I only wish I could have participated in in a movie or a play; but, not real life.

Talk about exhausted; traveling, meeting with detectives, meeting at the school, our next stop was Currie's Funeral Home in Henning, Tennessee, so that I could make funeral arrangements to prepare my son's body to be laid to rest later on in the week. I have to give a special thanks to my Uncle Frank Currie the owner of Currie's Funeral Home for helping me through this unbearable and unfamiliar

God's Purpose FOR MY PAIN

process that was just too much for me to handle alone. His love for me and my son as his family was evident with the kindness, sympathy and support shown for me. In his professionalism as a funeral director, he had already picked up JaRon's body from the coroner's officer in Memphis, Tennessee and assisted me in picking out JaRon's casket and finalizing the funeral arrangements for a memorial service to be held in the gymnasium at Ripley High School in Tennessee.

On Thursday August 4, 2011 from 1pm-5pm JaRon's friends, teachers, and teammates who would not have been able to travel to Indianapolis, Indiana for JaRon's formal funeral service, were able to pay their respects and see their friend before his body being transported to Indianapolis. Due to the fact that I wasn't able to sit through 2 funeral services, because I barley had the strength to make the arrangements and view his body before the public viewing; we left Tennessee on August 3rd, the day prior to the viewing in the gymnasium.

Before leaving Tennessee, we stopped by to visit my mother, Willadean Barbee, my Grandmother, Lossie M. Hayes, my Aunt Barbara J. Driver and Uncle Bumbardy Driver Jr.

During this visit at my aunt and uncle's house, Janice Broach from Channel 5 news out of Memphis, Tennessee wanted to do a news interview with the family seeking assistance in an attempt to find out who murdered JaRon. Because I was still so distraught, not able to speak, and did not want to try and think about what to say, or how to say it, JaRon's godmother, Indianapolis Metropolitan Detective Marta Bell did the television news interview; which was a plead to the community in the Tennessee area, for anyone who may have seen or heard anything or had any kind of information pertaining to the shooting murder of JaRon Collins to please contact the police department with that information.

THE JOURNEY CONTINUES

It's finally time to leave Ripley, Tennessee and head back to Indianapolis, Indiana to finalize the second funeral arrangements with Willaims and Bluitt Funeral Home in Indianapolis, Indiana. While traveling back to Indianapolis, I received a phone call from Detective Jim Joyner stating that they had arrested Terrance Moses as a suspect in my son's murder. I just started crying tears of joy and thankfulness. While I was grateful to God that this perpetrator and murderer had been caught, another part of me was still angry. Because I have served in a law enforcement capacity for years, a part of me wanted to turn around, go meet this menace to society and ask him why he took my son's life, and deal with him myself. At this point I have many emotions going on inside of me until I just don't know what to do or how to feel; so, I'm back at square one. Crying out to God saying Jesus Help me please I can't do this anymore, I'm falling apart. God spoke to me and said, no, you are not, I got you just continue to trust In the Lord with All Your Heart and Lean Not to Thy Own Understanding, In all Thy Ways Acknowledge Him and He will Direct Thy Path. (Proverbs 3:5)

I thank God for His Grace and Mercy Daily. I would like to thank my best friend, Marta Bell who is also JaRon's God Mother for standing by me and with me through this whole unbelievable and unbearable ordeal in the loss of our beloved JaRon E. Collins. Marta helped me by going to make funeral arrangements again at Williams and Bluitt Funeral Home because even though my son had been embalmed and dressed already by Currie's Funeral Home in Tennessee there was still preparation for his body to come in to Williams and Bluitt funeral Home in Indianapolis.

The Order of JaRon's Funeral Service

August 6, 2011

Mt. Vernon Missionary Baptist Church

709 N. Belmont Ave.

Indianapolis, Indiana 46222

11am – 1pm Viewing

1pm Funeral.

God's Purpose FOR MY PAIN

And God will wipe away every tear from their eyes; there shall be no more death, nor sorrow, nor crying. There shall be no more pain, for the former things have passed away. (Revelations 21:4)

A special thanks to my Uncle Frank Currie of Currie's Funeral Home in Henning, Tennessee for allowing my son's body to be transported to Indianapolis, Indiana and delivered to Williams and Bluitt Funeral Home by Funeral Directors Allan Baldon, my cousin and Johnnie Mae Currie my aunt. The day has come for me and my family to pay our respect to my baby boy JaRon. I can't wrap my mind around the fact that I am about to attend his funeral. This just can't be real, this has got to be a bad dream that I just need to wake up from. As the limo arrived to my house to pick up me and my family and take us to our church, enroute to the church, I just wanted to pass out so I didn't have to deal with this day of putting my son's body to rest. Lord help me I cried out as they helped me out of the limo and escorted me into the church. The closer they escorted me to the front of our church where my son's body laid in his casket, the heavier my legs and feet were, I felt like weights were on my ankles weighing me down and I didn't want to even deal with saying my final goodbyes to my son.

One after one, after one, after one, family, friends, and my Law Enforcement Family marched around to view my son's body and hugged me; but, I was so numb, I don't even remember half of the people that were there. I just know that I was in so much pain and I wanted to just get inside that casket with my son because I couldn't let him leave me like this. It wasn't fair; I needed him here with me because I didn't want to live without my baby. What was I going to do? Lord Please Help Me…..Jesus, Jesus, Jesus, this is so hard is all I could scream out and say while the choir sang. Remarks were spoken and read and as the minister began to eulogize my son, I continued to plead with the Lord, begging him to PLEASE! let me have my son back. My son is an innocent child with a lot of life left to live, he didn't do anything to deserve laying here in this casket…take me Lord, take me, I pleaded.

Now, as the Funeral Director of Williams and Bluitt, Mr. James Dixon III prepared to close the casket so that we could head to the gravesite, the reality of everything started to hit me all over again. My baby is gone and I can't see him anymore; so, I cried, screamed, prayed, prayed, screamed, and cried as I said my final goodbye.

We are now enroute to the Crown Hill Cemetery where my son will be laid to rest. My son's funeral procession was escorted by Indianapolis Metropolitan Police Department Police Cars and Motorcycle Traffic Units along with the Marion County Sheriff's Office honor Guard Team, Bagpipers. Once we made it to the entrance of the Cemetery, standing by for our arrival was the Indianapolis Metropolitan Police Department Motorcycle Units, Bike Unit, and fellow patrol Officers that I work with and who daily supported me through the difficult loss of my son.

Now that this journey has come to the final end of my son's resting place and I can't go any further with him, reality had set in when the minister gave his finally remarks and they began to lower my baby's casket into the ground. I felt my heart stop beating for a brief moment and they had to physically remove me from the cemetery because I just wanted to stay there with my son. I didn't want to leave him and I felt I had died with him and that life was over for me also.

How would I ever be able to get my life back to normal without my son? Once all my family and friends go back to their lives, it will just be me at home by myself, missing my son. See, it's one thing to have everyone there with you when you are going through your storm; but, when they leave, the phone calls stop, what do I do now? Because, the storm is still raging and I don't know who to turn to our what to do. BUT GOD!

THE STRUGGLE IS REAL

Moving forward 2 months after JaRon's death and I'm still really struggling. I'm off work because I just couldn't go back to work at that time; being a Police Officer and trying to deal with any death or homicide or taking runs, my mind, body, nor spirit were not ready for that; especially if any of those dispatched runs would require me to deal with a young person, I felt that would probably send me overboard and cause me to relive the tragic death of my son; so, I just didn't want to take that chance, nor be around any police related matters at that time.

I was just home alone, frustrated, hurting, and crying out to God about how lonely I was for my son, because I missed him dearly. I even found myself driving to his graveside every day and just crying out to God about how much I missed JaRon and that I couldn't live without him not being at home with me.

On September 11, 2011 I had a really bad emotional meltdown about 3:00 am and I'm crying out to God because I was in such a dark place and wanted to make Terrance Moses pay for the hurt and pain that he caused me and my family. And, guess what? The devil was busy planting ungodly things in my head about how I could get even with Terrance Moses for killing my son, about how I could make him experience some of the same hurt and pain that

he had caused me and my family; BUT GOD…..
God spoke to me and said call your friend Pastor
Darryl E. Davis Sr. I had met Pastor Davis prior to
my son's death, I had visited his church and we were
friends and I talked to him occasionally on the phone.
But, I didn't think it was a good ideal to call him at
3am in the morning; but, God stayed on me until I
finally picked up the phone and called him. Pastor
Davis answered the phone on the first ring and
because I was crying and so distraught Pastor Davis
immediately started praying for me; and, after he
prayed he said look Lossie, I don't know what you are
going through because I have never lost a child, but
God told me to tell you that everything is going to be
alright, and he stayed on the phone with me until It
was time for him to be at work at the Marion County
Health Department, which was 6am. Pastor Davis

checked on my periodically throughout the day and from that day forward Pastor Davis and I became really close. On July 14, 2012 Pastor Davis proposed to me and told me that the morning that I call him crying out to him about how devastated I was over the loss of my son JaRon, he said it was then that God told him that I was going to be his wife, and I laughed and said wow, well I wish God had have told me that you were going to be my husband because I sure wasn't looking for one. That's why they say "be careful what you ask and pray for" because when I was crying out to God about how lonely I was in missing my son, God heard my cry and sent me a wonderful man of God, not to replace my son; but, to fill that void and to help me spiritually to get myself together so I could learn how to live without my son in the flesh, because my son will always live in my heart.

Lossie M. Davis

Restored Peace

Lord, you will establish peace for us, For you have also done all our works in us (Isaiah 26:12)

Now that I was trying to piece together my life without my son, I received a phone call from Detective Jim Joyner of the Dyersburg Police Department and District Attorney Phillip Bivens stating that the murder trial for Terrance Moses would start August 6, 2012. Almost 1-year to the date of JaRon's death and I just wasn't prepared to have to relive my son's death all over again; but, I wanted justice to be served so my family and I could have some closure. My family, friends, and my fiancé Pastor Darryl E. Davis Sr., traveled to Tennessee with me as my support system to help me deal with going through the process of getting Terrance Moses convicted for the murder of my beloved son JaRon. I knew this murder trial was going to devastate me all over again; rehashing details of how my son was shot down in cold blood for no reason but, I also knew that it was something that I had to go through not just for closure for me and my family; but, for justice and to honor my son whose life was cut short at the hands of this violent defendant.

The trial went on for one week; testimony after testimony, witness after witness, sitting through long hours of court testimonies, from 8:00 am till 6:00 pm every evening for the entire week, this was so draining. On Friday, the last day of the trial, the jury had finally reached a verdict.......GUILTY!

It took the jury in the murder trial case against Terrance Moses for killing my 17 year old son, JaRon, 29 minutes to convict him of FIRST DEGREE MURDER! WITH LIFE IN PRISON! WITHOUT THE POSSIBILITY OF PAROLE......JUSTICE!

I was so excited and relieved to know that this animal would never be able to walk the streets of Tennessee or anywhere else in the world and terrorize anyone else's family by destroying their life like he had done mine and my family.

I recall that the entire week that Terrance Moses was sitting in that courtroom, he had this unnerving - smirk/smile on his face, that instantly went away when he was read his murder conviction. He had never showed any remorse in the courtroom or to me and my family for what he had done; shooting my unarmed, innocent child in the back and killing him in a case of mistaken identity. The tables had turned, in our favor, and me and my family now had the closure that we deserved; and I had the strength and was able to give a statement to the television News Reporter, Jason Cannon; whereas before, I was unable to speak. This time through the victory of a guilty verdict and a sentence of life without parole, God granted me the strength to publicly say to Terrance Moses "I forgive you for killing my son because in order for God to forgive me I have to forgive you. And, I pray that God has mercy on your soul because only God can give life and take life and you had no right to take my son's life. You robbed me of his future. I will never get to see him graduate high school, college, become a productive citizen, get married or have children because you took that away from me. So, I pray that every day you take a breath, you think about JaRon my son, who can't take a breath anymore due to your senseless act of violence that took his life.

I don't know if you have family who loved or cared about you; but JaRon's family loved him dearly; even though God loved him more because he's in God's care now. JaRon is being a guardian angel over me as I go on with my life back out on the streets as a Police Officer, dealing with fools like you every day that have no regard for human life.

As I tried to move forward and deal daily with the loss of my son, I realized that God had placed Pastor Darryl E. Davis Sr., in my life to help me spiritually deal with the loss of JaRon. While he could never replace my son, his care and concern and love for me has helped fill that void of loneliness that I kept crying out to God about.

On April 6, 2013 Darryl E. Davis Sr., became my husband and he now pastors Ambassador Baptist Church located at 2301 N. Arsenal Avenue, Indianapolis, Indiana 46218.

All I can say is BUT GOD! Only God knows the reason why there is…. A PURPOSE FOR MY PAIN.

God makes no mistakes and can't no devil in hell steal my joy, because the joy that I have the world didn't give it to me and the world sure can't take it away unless I allow them to. And, I won't let anyone or the world do that because God has been too good to me. He saved me; He saved me from a burning hell where I was headed because He is a God of not just a second chance; but, another chance.

God's Purpose FOR MY PAIN

To God Be The Glory For All The Great Things He Has Done!

Thank you Lord for My Purpose. Thank you Lord for My Pain. I won't complain, I trust you.

LOVE. LOSS. LAW.

REFLECTIONS

As I look back over my life, the death of my precious son at the age of 17; that I carried in my womb for 9 months is by far the most difficult and devastating situation that I have ever been in and gone through in my life; and, trust me when I say that I have been through some things in this life time.

As a person who chose Law Enforcement as a career and spending almost 15 years as a police officer prior to my son's death I knew I was human and went through the same things that people do who we have been sworn to protect and serve daily.

Citizens who don't live in or understand the world of law enforcement seem to think that we as police are exempt from being victims of crime and experiencing the same hurts and pains as others.

Imagine devoting your life, as I have, to protecting and serving citizens and keeping their homes and children's and lives safe and out of the hands of criminals and then you're facing just what you are working so hard against for other people, not to become victims of crimes perpetrated upon them by the criminal element. My son was murdered, my son JaRon was not a thug, he was a loving son and a normal 17 year old teenager, going to school, an honor roll student, playing basketball, and preparing to graduate from high school the next year as a senior and looking forward to going to college.

JaRon had an infectious smile that had you hooked the first time you saw him; and while he did have a girlfriend, just like most 17 year olds, the girls were popular with him and he was popular with everyone; his teachers, basketball coaches, and friends alike.

In Love I birthed Jaron,

In Loss-JaRon was murdered.

In Law- I am still committed to protect and serve.

From the heart and soul of a grieving mother who prays that violence in every state, North, South East, and West would stop and that people would turn to God and turn away from their wicked and violent ways.

Lossie M. Davis, A servant of God with a forgiving and loving heart.

www.ingramcontent.com/pod-product-compliance
Lightning Source LLC
LaVergne TN
LVHW051203080426
835508LV00021B/2773